I ♥ LOVE MY QUEER KID

·····

＊Ａ＊

WORKBOOK TO AFFIRM
AND SUPPORT YOUR
LGBTQ+ CHILD OR TEEN

MARC CAMPBELL, LMHC

SKILLS TO CHANGE YOUR LIFE AND THE...
www.Microcosm.Pub
2752 N WILLIAMS AVE · PORTLAND, OR 97227

Portland, OR | Cleveland, OH

I Love My Queer Kid: A Workbook to Affirm and Support Your LGBTQ+ Child or Teen

© Marc Campbell, 2023

This edition © Microcosm Publishing, 2023

This edition first published November 7, 2023

Cover & design by Joe Biel

Edited by Olivia Rollins

ISBN 9781648412301

This is Microcosm #792

For a catalog, write or visit:

Microcosm Publishing

2752 N Williams Ave.

Portland, OR 97227

(503)799-2698

www.Microcosm.Pub/ILoveMyQueerKid

To join the ranks of high-class stores that feature Microcosm titles, talk to your rep: In the U.S. **Como** (Atlantic), **Abraham** (Midwest), **Third Act** (Texas, Oklahoma, Louisiana, Arkansas), **Imprint** (Pacific), **Turnaround** in Europe, **Manda/UTP** in Canada, **New South** in Australia. We are sold in the gift market by **Faire** and **Emerald.**

Global labor conditions are bad, and our roots in industrial Cleveland in the '70s and '80s made us appreciate the need to treat workers right. Therefore, our books are MADE IN THE USA.

MICROCOSM · PUBLISHING

About the Publisher

MICROCOSM PUBLISHING is Portland's most diversified publishing house and distributor, with a focus on the colorful, authentic, and empowering. Our books and zines have put your power in your hands since 1996, equipping readers to make positive changes in their lives and in the world around them. Microcosm emphasizes skill-building, showing hidden histories, and fostering creativity through challenging conventional publishing wisdom with books and bookettes about DIY skills, food, bicycling, gender, self-care, and social justice. What was once a distro and record label started by Joe Biel in a drafty bedroom was determined to be *Publishers Weekly*'s fastest-growing publisher of 2022 and #3 in 2023, and is now among the oldest independent publishing houses in Portland, OR, and Cleveland, OH. We are a politically moderate, centrist publisher in a world that has inched to the right for the past 80 years.

Contents

⌁Introduction⌁

Y ou did it: you started the journey. Sometimes that is the hardest step; just starting this workbook means that you acknowledge that you could use some help when it comes to handling your child's coming out as queer or trans. Unfortunately, that is so much more than millions of parents around the world can do. You love your child, and it is okay if you feel uncomfortable, overwhelmed, or blindsided since they came out. It is okay if you're not quite sure how to parent your child. The important part is your willingness to learn and grow. This workbook will challenge you to look within, expand your thinking, and act.

First of all, what your child is going through is completely normal, and it took an incredible amount of courage for them to come out. It speaks volumes that your child felt safe enough to share a personal part of their identity. Or maybe this wasn't the case; maybe your child didn't come out to you, but you found out another way. Regardless, you are taking a great step towards having a closer relationship with your child.

This workbook, which is designed to be completed over nine weeks, is for anyone who has a child in their life who recently came out or was outed by other means. While most of the content will address you as a "parent," it's not just for parents: you will also benefit from the exercises if the LGBTQ+ child in your life is your grandchild, foster child, or younger sibling. This workbook is for people at all different levels of comfort with and understanding of LGBTQ+ issues, sexuality, and gender identity. The content is primarily geared towards children (of all ages), but this workbook can also be helpful if your child is an adult.

You can tailor the various exercises to better suit your child's age and your relationship with them. Your engagement with this workbook, and the lessons you take away from it, could vary a lot based on these factors and more. For example, a conversation about your child's friendships would look a lot different with a 5-year-old than with a 17-year-old. And if you are working through this workbook because you want to better support your LGBTQ+ grandchild, foster child, or other family member, you can tailor your reflections and responses based on the nature of your relationship with them.

And finally, even if you haven't had a child come out to you yet, this workbook will equip you with helpful tools that you can use if this happens in the future. The important thing is that you engage with this workbook in the way that will be most beneficial to you and will help you grow in your understanding and acceptance of LGBTQ+ youth.

Why This Book Is Needed

The percentage of people in Gen Z and younger identifying as part of the LGBTQ+ community is growing more and more each year. Fortunately, this is mainly due to the world becoming more accepting of queer people. Unfortunately, it doesn't mean that the world is completely safe for us. The number one cause of death for LGBTQ+ children is suicide. That needs repeating: the number one cause of death for LGBTQ+ children is suicide. The number one prevention for that suicide is a parent that provides a loving, understanding, and accepting environment for their child.

This workbook can help give you the tools and knowledge to offer that support to your kid. Countless children who come out feel overwhelmed, helpless, and exhausted trying to explain their sexuality and gender identity—trying to explain who they are—to their parents. This can take a negative toll on your child's mental health and can potentially lead to self-harm or suicide. This workbook helps to take some of the pressure off the child and redirect it to the parent.

Who I Am

As a queer person, a former middle school counselor, and a licensed mental health counselor in the state of Florida, I not only have personal experience with the coming-out process, but I also have thousands of hours of experience helping queer and trans youth through the challenges that come with living in a world that doesn't fully accept all parts of their identities. Time and time again, I have provided therapy for queer and trans kids and they have shared similar stories of emotional distress caused by their parents, some intentional, some not. My hope is to help queer and trans children not only in therapy sessions but also at home through educating their parents. Home is where they need the most support, and that's why I created this workbook.

Things You Should Know

The language used throughout the book might not be familiar or comfortable for you; that is intentional. One of the goals of this workbook is to help you feel more comfortable with using new terminology. There is growth in discomfort.

For example, throughout the workbook I will use the term "queer" to describe your child and people in the LGBTQ+ community. I use this term because I don't know how your child identifies and queer is an empowering (to some) umbrella term to use for people of many different sexual orientations and gender identities. It can be helpful to take language cues from your child and other queer people in your life, take note of the words and phrases they use, and ask questions on why they use those words and whether it is okay for you to use them as well.

This workbook is made to push you; you are not going to enjoy everything you read or every activity. Here are some tips for when you feel uncomfortable or triggered while working through a section of this workbook (this list is in no way exhaustive):

1. Check in with your body. For some it can be harder to identify thoughts and feelings you are experiencing in the moment. It could be helpful to check in with your physiological response, such as your heart rate, muscle tension, and breathing.

2. Identify what specific part of the workbook caused an emotional response. For example, was the content addressing sexuality or gender? Was it focused on you or your child?

3. Refer to your list of coping skills (see Week 1) and pick one coping skill to engage in.

4. Lean into your support system: friends, family, and community.

5. If you aren't already in therapy, consider finding a mental health therapist and starting to work with them. Look up therapists who are LGBTQ+ or LGBTQ+ affirming.

Some topics addressed will not directly relate to your child's identity. However, it is important to complete all the pages to help build knowledge, respect, and acceptance of the whole LGBTQ+ community.

Some of the exercises say, "Write your thoughts and feelings." These words are intentional. Each time you see this, make sure to include your thoughts **and** feelings. Thought: "The weather is so nice today." Feelings:

"Happy, calm, thankful." A lot of times, things are processed through thoughts **or** feelings; however, to get a fuller picture, it is important to process both. This will lead to a better understanding of yourself and will help you get much more out of this workbook.

Whether your child is aware that you are engaging with this workbook or not, there is a risk that they will find it and look through it. Since you are in a process of growth and this workbook requires you to explore some of your raw, unedited thoughts and feelings about your child's identity, some of your responses could potentially cause emotional damage if your child reads them. Therefore, it is crucial that you hide the workbook so your child won't find it. If your child does find this workbook and reads any part of it, it will be important to have a conversation with them about it. Explain that this workbook is for your own personal growth, that you're working through it because you love them and want to better support them, and that the thoughts and feelings you express in it aren't permanent.

Special Assignments

This workbook includes a variety of worksheets, exercises, and challenges for you to complete. Here are some to look out for.

Special Challenge: These challenges are meant to push you out of your comfort zone. One of the best ways to grow emotionally is to expose yourself to new experiences. If you are not ready for one of these challenges when you come across it, make note of this and see if you are able to reattempt the challenge at a later time.

Let's Talk: These are conversational prompts to help increase communication, openness, and understanding between you and your child.

Timed Worksheets: These are quick timed exercises designed to help increase your awareness of some of your more automatic thoughts and biases.

End-of-Week Reflections: When you reach the end of each week, you will be asked to pause and consider what you have learned. This is to make sure that you do not rush through the process. When you get to this page, take that day to review previous pages and reflect on your growth. These pages also include space for you to take notes for the week.

Key Terminology

Here is a list of key terms pertaining to the LGBTQ+ community. This list is not exhaustive but will help lay a foundation of knowledge. As you work through this workbook, refer back to these definitions as needed.

Agender: Describes individuals that do not identify with a particular gender. Genderfree and genderless are other terms sometimes used.

Aromantic: Describes individuals that have zero to little romantic attraction towards others. They might not have the desire to be in a romantic relationship. It is a common misconception that aromantic people do not have sexual desires; many aromantic people do enjoy and engage in sex.

Asexual: Describes individuals that have zero to little sexual attraction towards others. It is a common misconception that asexual people don't engage in sexual activities; asexual people do engage in sexual activities for various reasons.

Bisexual: Describes individuals that experience attraction (romantic and/or sexual) towards multiple genders. Some people feel that the term excludes those that don't identify as a man or a woman. However, many bisexual people are attracted to nonbinary people.

Cisgender (cis): Describes individuals that do not go through a mental, social, and/or physical transition of their gender identity. Like trans people, cis people might change their gender expression throughout life.

Femme/masc: Terms used by queer people, typically in addition to sexual orientation and gender identity, to help describe themselves. Femme describes a feminine gender expression, while masc describes a masculine gender expression. For example, lesbians might describe themselves as femme or masc, which might key other queer people into their gender expression or identity.

Gay: Describes individuals that experience attraction (romantic and/or sexual) towards someone of the same gender. This term is typically used to describe men; however, many individuals in the LGBTQ+ community use "gay" to describe themselves.

Gender dysphoria: *The Diagnostic and Statistical Manual of Mental Disorders* defines this as "marked incongruence between [an individual's] experienced or expressed gender and the one they were assigned at birth." This could cause anxiety and discomfort. Many things can trigger gender dysphoria; for some, being misgendered (referred to by the wrong pronouns) can cause dysphoria, while for others it can be triggered by simply looking in the mirror.

Gender expression: How individuals express their gender, usually through outward appearance (clothing and hair), though it is not limited to that.

Gender identity: An individual's sense of their gender and self. Gender identity can lean masculine, feminine, both, or neither; it can also be static or fluid.

Genderfluid: Describes individuals that do not have a static gender identity. The frequency of the change in gender identity can vary; for example, it might fluctuate every day or every few months.

Gender-nonconforming: Describes an individual that does not conform to society's expectation of their gender expression or identity.

Genderqueer: An umbrella term used for individuals who have gender identities outside of the gender binary (woman/man).

Homophobia: Fear, discomfort, dislike, and hatred towards queer people.

Intersex: Describes individuals with sex chromosomes, reproductive systems, or genitalia that's considered neither typically male nor typically female. Being intersex is naturally occurring and does not necessarily call for any medical intervention.

Lesbian: A woman that is attracted (romantically and/or sexually) to other women. Many individuals of varying gender identities (nonbinary, genderqueer, and more) can also identify as lesbians.

Nonbinary: Describes individuals who have a gender identity that does not fit within the gender binary (woman/man). Many nonbinary people do not identify as trans, but some do.

Pansexual: Describes individuals that experience attraction regardless of a person's gender identity or biological sex.

Queer: An umbrella term used to describe people that do not identify as heterosexual and/or cisgender. Many feel the term is empowering and inclusive. Some gay, lesbian, bisexual, and transgender people also use the term "queer" to describe themselves.

Questioning: Describes individuals who are unsure of or exploring their sexuality and/or gender identity.

Transgender: Describes individuals that go through a mental, social, and/or physical transition of their gender identity. It is important to note that many trans people do not go through a medical transition. For many, a social transition (e.g., changing their name, gender expression, and pronouns) leads to great life satisfaction.

Transphobia: Fear, discomfort, dislike, and hatred towards transgender people. Trans people are the most vulnerable in the LGBTQ+ community when it comes to hate crimes.

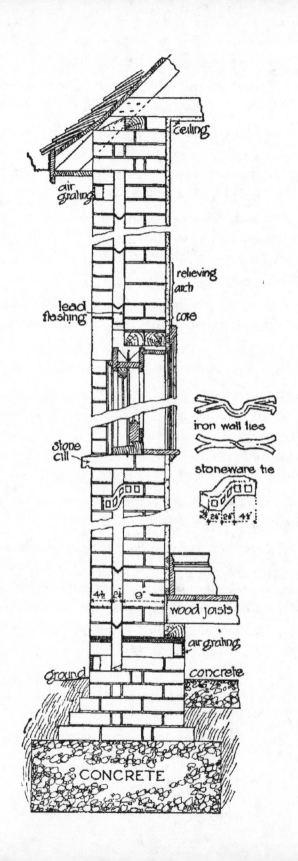

ceiling

air grating

relieving arch

lead flashing

core

iron wall ties

stoneware tie

2" 2½" 2½" 4½"

stone cill

4½" 2½" 9"

wood joists

air grating

ground

concrete

CONCRETE

Week 1: Laying Foundations

Because this is going to be a challenge.

*T*he focus of Week 1 is to help you set your intentions, to offer you coping skills in case things become overwhelming or triggering, and to help you keep your child safe. Setting your intentions helps to add focus and clarity to your reflections and responses, and the coping skills you will learn this week will become more helpful in the coming weeks as some of the topics become more difficult and personal. Safety, meanwhile, should always be the top priority, which is why we're including it in this first week.

Setting Intentions

Setting intentions is a great way to get the most out of this workbook. When you set intentions, you are reminding yourself of your purpose, your "why."

I bought this workbook because I hope to . . .

_____

_____

_____

I am ready to start this journey of growth because . . .

_____

_____

_____

Reflect on the answers you wrote for the previous two questions, then write three goals you hope to achieve by completing this workbook.

_____

_____

_____

Coping Skills

Many questions and exercises in this workbook could potentially be triggering. They could bring to the front of your mind any traumas you have experienced or feelings of sadness and discomfort. This section is meant to prepare you for this possibility by exploring your coping skills. Coping skills are simply ways in which you cope with any uncomfortable feelings you are experiencing. They look different for everyone and could have different levels of impact. This section also includes some breathing and grounding exercises that you can return to later if you feel triggered or emotionally drained by any part of this workbook.

List the coping skills you engage in to distract yourself from your feelings:

_____

_____

List the coping skills you engage in to process your feelings (e.g., journaling, drawing, music):

_____

_____

List the coping skills you engage in when you feel sad:

_____

_____

List the coping skills you engage in when you feel angry:

_____

_____

List the coping skills you engage in that are not helpful to your mental health:

_____

_____

_____

Breathing and Visualization

Just in case it was challenging to come up with your coping skills, you are going to learn two simple ones now: deep breathing and visualization. The twist is that you are going to edit them to fit your needs.

Start with the classic 4-7-8 breathing technique:

Breathe in through your nose for a count of **four**.

Hold the breath for a count of **seven**.

Part your lips and exhale loudly for a count of **eight**.

Now create your own timing, then write down what felt the best for you:

Breathe in through your nose for a count of _____

Hold the breath for a count of _____

Part your lips and exhale loudly for a count of _____

Now you will incorporate visualization. Imagine a relaxing location; it can be a place you have been before, a place you want to visit, or a fictional location. What do you see? Imagine the sounds: Do you hear a gentle melody or soothing waves? Imagine the smells: Is there the scent of fresh-baked cookies or lavender? Take your time to decide on the details of your location, then write those down.

_____

_____

_____

_____

_____

_____

_____

_____

_____

_____

_____

_____

_____

_____

_____

_____

_____

_____

_____

_____

_____

Time to practice. Review the details of your deep breathing and visualization, then practice each coping skill. After you practice, answer the reflection questions below.

What was it like to practice the deep-breathing exercise? How did you feel afterward?

_____

_____

_____

_____

_____

_____

_____

_____

_____

_____

_____

_____

_____

What was it like to practice the visualization exercise? How did you feel afterward?

_____

_____

_____

_____

_____

_____

_____

_____

_____

_____

_____

_____

_____

Self-Care List

List three to five activities that bring you joy.

_____

_____

_____

_____

List three to five activities that bring you calm.

_____

_____

_____

_____

List three to five activities you can do by yourself.

_____

_____

_____

_____

List three to five activities you could do with others.

_____

_____

_____

_____

List three to five activities you could do with your child.

_____

_____

_____

_____

Queer Comfort Assessment: Baseline

The Queer Comfort Assessment is a tool created to help you examine your own biases. Think of the Queer Comfort Assessment as a mirror. A mirror does not judge, it just offers a reflection. Try to be honest with yourself; you might be surprised or upset by some of your responses, and that's okay. Try not to judge yourself, because the person you are today, filling out this assessment, will not be the same as the person who emerges at the end of these nine weeks. You will retake the Queer Comfort Assessment at the midpoint of this workbook and again at the end to help track your learning and growth.

I am comfortable seeing two men kissing on television.

○ *strongly disagree* ○ *disagree* ○ *neutral* ○ *agree* ○ *strongly agree*

I am comfortable using "they/them" pronouns for anyone that asks.

○ *strongly disagree* ○ *disagree* ○ *neutral* ○ *agree* ○ *strongly agree*

I would be okay with wearing the clothing of a different gender outside.

○ *strongly disagree* ○ *disagree* ○ *neutral* ○ *agree* ○ *strongly agree*

I am comfortable going to a pride parade.

○ *strongly disagree* ○ *disagree* ○ *neutral* ○ *agree* ○ *strongly agree*

I am comfortable attending a drag show or event.

○ *strongly disagree* ○ *disagree* ○ *neutral* ○ *agree* ○ *strongly agree*

I am comfortable going to an LGBTQ+ bar.

○ *strongly disagree* ○ *disagree* ○ *neutral* ○ *agree* ○ *strongly agree*

Children are capable of knowing their sexuality.

○ *strongly disagree* ○ *disagree* ○ *neutral* ○ *agree* ○ *strongly agree*

I am comfortable with a boy dressing as a Disney princess for Halloween.

○ *strongly disagree* ○ *disagree* ○ *neutral* ○ *agree* ○ *strongly agree*

I am comfortable with trans teens taking hormones to transition (e.g., estrogen or testosterone).

○ *strongly disagree* ○ *disagree* ○ *neutral* ○ *agree* ○ *strongly agree*

I have questioned my own sexuality.

○ *strongly disagree* ○ *disagree* ○ *neutral* ○ *agree* ○ *strongly agree*

I have questioned my own gender identity.

○ *strongly disagree* ○ *disagree* ○ *neutral* ○ *agree* ○ *strongly agree*

How to Calculate Results

Strongly disagree: 1 point

Disagree: 2 points

Neutral: 3 points

Agree: 4 points

Strongly agree: 5 points

Your result: _____

11–27 points: Heteronormality has made queerness very uncomfortable for you. You have a ways to go, but starting the journey is what's most important.

28–39 points: You have some discomfort with queerness, but you do have a level of tolerance that can easily be built on.

40–49 points: You are mostly comfortable with queerness. More exposure will lead to a lot of growth.

50+ points: You are completely comfortable with queerness!

Your results should only be used to increase your self-awareness; they are in no way an indication of your character.

Processing

How did you feel about your responses on the Queer Comfort Assessment? Write your thoughts and feelings.

_____

_____

_____

_____

_____

_____

_____

_____

_____

_____

_____

_____

_____

_____

_____

_____

_____

If you completed the Queer Comfort Assessment 10 years ago, would any of your responses differ? Which ones and why?

_____

_____

_____

_____

_____

_____

_____

_____

_____

_____

_____

_____

_____

_____

_____

_____

Do you foresee any of these responses changing in the future? Which ones and why?

_____

_____

_____

_____

_____

_____

Safety

When a child comes out, many parents begin to worry about their physical and emotional safety. That is probably one of the many reasons you purchased this workbook. Unfortunately, we live in an imperfect world that includes bigotry and violence.

Physical safety is prevention of bodily harm—maintaining physical wellness.

Emotional safety is prevention of emotional harm—maintaining mental wellness.

List some ways in which you keep your child physically safe, such as household rules or precautions you take.

_____

_____

_____

_____

_____

_____

Did any of your methods of keeping your child physically safe change since your child came out? If so, how?

_____

_____

_____

_____

_____

_____

Do you believe your child's physical safety is more at risk since they came out? If so, how?

_____

_____

_____

_____

_____

_____

_____

List some ways in which you keep your child emotionally safe. For example, not cussing in front of your child, using kind words, and checking in about bullying.

_____

_____

_____

_____

_____

_____

_____

Was it harder for you to think of ways you keep your child physically safe or ways you keep your child emotionally safe?

○ *Physical Safety* | ○ *Emotional Safety*

Do you believe your child is more worried about their physical safety or their emotional safety?

○ *Physical Safety* | ○ *Emotional Safety*

Write down some of your thoughts and feelings about your child's safety since they came out. Also, write some of your ideas on how you can keep your child physically and emotionally safe.

_____

_____

_____

_____

_____

_____

_____

_____

_____

_____

_____

_____

_____

_____

_____

_____

_____

_____

_____

_____

Some Tips to Keep Your Child Physically Safe

- Don't panic; keep doing what you have been doing. You have kept your child physically safe their whole life.

- If applicable, read the policies of the school district your child attends. Check their policies on bullying and LGBTQ+ students.

- Ask your child if they feel safe at home, school, extracurricular activities, and work, if applicable. Gather as much information as possible. Ask if there are any people they feel uncomfortable or unsafe around.

Some Tips to Keep Your Child Emotionally Safe

- Keep an open channel of communication. Check in with your child not only by asking "How are you feeling?" but also with more specific questions. Some examples are "What are some things you are worried about?" and "Is there anything I can help you with?" Questions like these aren't normally asked by parents, which is exactly why it is important to ask your queer child these questions.

- Ask for support. If your child has a school counselor, call or email them. They can meet with your child and even teach them some tools to cope with overwhelming feelings.

- This one is the same as one of the tips for keeping your child physically safe: If applicable, read the policies of the school district your child attends. Check their policies on bullying and LGBTQ+ students.

- Ask your child if they would like to start therapy services. Let them know that they can help with the process of choosing a therapist; make sure to focus searches on therapists who are LGBTQ+ affirming and allied.

Physical and Emotional Safety Action Plan

Now you will have a discussion with your child about safety. To make sure your child doesn't happen to read other pages of your workbook, write down the responses on a separate sheet of paper, then copy them over to your workbook for your review. This list is in no way exhaustive; you can make adjustments or skip some of the steps so that it fits the needs of your child.

1. Ask your child if they have any concerns about their safety.

_____

_____

_____

_____

2. Ask your child if they feel safe at school (or any other relevant locations).

_____

_____

_____

_____

3. Explore what "emotional safety" means to your child. Write down a definition.

_____

_____

_____

_____

4. Work with your child to create a list of trusted people (adults and peers included) that your child can talk to if they feel physically unsafe.

_____

_____

_____

_____

_____

_____

5. Work with your child to create a list of trusted people that your child can talk to if they feel emotionally unsafe.

_____

_____

_____

_____

_____

_____

6. Contact your child's school counselor to ask for periodic mental health check-ins for your child. Ask for your child's permission to share intimate details with the school counselor.

7. If your child is interested, work with them to decide on a mental health counselor they could meet with to build rapport and so they can add another trusted person to their lists. They do not have to commit to consistent therapy sessions; this meeting is for your child to build comfort.

8. Ask your child if there is anything you could do to help them feel more safe, both physically and emotionally.

_____

_____

_____

_____

_____

_____

_____

_____

_____

_____

_____

Suicide Safety Plan

This is a helpful template you can use to create a suicide safety plan with your child. Before you follow this template, ask your child if they are experiencing suicidal thoughts; if not, then you can skip this section. As with the previous exercise, write down your child's responses to the safety plan on a separate sheet of paper, then copy them over to your workbook for your review. Depending on your child's age, it could be helpful to make a copy for them to keep to refer to if they are feeling suicidal. Most likely, this will be developmentally appropriate for children 12 years old and up, but not always; use your best judgment. If your child is younger than 12 and has expressed suicidal ideation, it would be helpful for them to have a copy.

Record your child's responses to the following prompts:

Three people (peers and adults) you trust to talk to about your suicidal thoughts:

_____

_____

_____

Three activities you can do by yourself that help you feel calm and/or happy:

_____

_____

_____

Three activities you can do with others that help you feel calm and/or happy:

_____

_____

_____

Professionals or agencies you can contact during an emotional crisis:

_____

_____

_____

Ways you can remove access to harmful items in your environment:

_____

_____

_____

_____

One thing you are looking forward to in the next six months **or** one thing you can plan to do in the next six months that you would look forward to:

_____

_____

_____

_____

_____

_____

_____

_____

_____

_____

_____

_____

_____

_____

_____

_____

_____

Take a pause.

You are doing great! Take a day or two off from the workbook. It is advised that you take some time to review previous pages and reflect on your progress before moving ahead. Remember, this is a journey, not a race. Use the following space to write down your reflections or take notes for the week.

_____

_____

_____

_____

_____

_____

_____

_____

_____

_____

_____

_____

_____

_____

_____

_____

_____

_____

_____

Week 2: Where You Are Coming From

Because you gotta start somewhere.

T his week is mostly about feelings . . . yay! You will reflect on your thoughts and feelings about your child's sexual orientation and/or gender identity. You will also reflect on your childhood experiences and your biases, many of which are formed in childhood.

What Do You Know?

Let's start with a quick exercise to see what you know about the LGBTQ+ community.

Timed Worksheet Alert!!

The following page is a timed worksheet. Get your phone out and set your timer to 60 seconds! This includes the time to read the instructions. Start the timer when you turn the page.

Ready . . . set . . . go!!

Timed Worksheet

Which letter(s) in the LGBTQ+ (lesbian, gay, bisexual, transgender, queer, and plus) community do you think you know the most about?

_____

Which letter(s) in the LGBTQ+ community do you think you know the least about?

_____

Processing

Why do you think you know more about certain letters in LGBTQ+ than others?

_____

_____

_____

_____

_____

_____

_____

_____

_____

What would you like to learn about the letters you are less familiar with?

_____

_____

_____

_____

_____

_____

_____

_____

Your Childhood Experiences

Reflecting on your own childhood can help build empathy about what your child is going through since they came out.

Describe your relationship with your parents/guardians growing up. Write your thoughts and feelings.

_____

_____

_____

_____

_____

_____

_____

_____

_____

_____

_____

_____

_____

_____

_____

_____

_____

_____

_____

How is your relationship with your child different from how your relationship with your parents was when you were a kid?

_____

_____

_____

_____

_____

_____

_____

_____

_____

_____

_____

_____

_____

_____

_____

_____

_____

_____

_____

_____

_____

_____

_____

What is your plan to create a household that is emotionally safe for your child to express their feelings? Will you take the same approach your parents did? Write your thoughts and feelings.

_____

_____

_____

_____

_____

_____

_____

_____

_____

_____

_____

_____

_____

Identifying Your Thoughts

Awareness is usually the first step towards any meaningful change. This exercise will help you increase your awareness. Try to complete this without any judgment towards your own thoughts; it's okay that you have them, and with more awareness, you can work to edit some of those thoughts.

Directions: Put a check next to any of the thoughts that you've had since your child came out.

○ He's just doing it for attention.

○ She's too young to know for sure.

○ I don't want his life to be harder.

○ He picked this up from TikTok.

○ They are just copying their friends.

○ Why does my child have to be _____?

○ He doesn't mean it . . . it's the cool thing to do nowadays . . .

○ This is just a phase.

○ What are my parents going to think?

○ I am glad she felt comfortable sharing that with me.

○ I am worried about their future.

○ I am worried about their safety.

○ I am not sure how to support him.

○ I hope he is doing okay.

○ I don't want to say the wrong thing.

○ What is the right thing to do?

"Check" Your Biases

This is another exercise to help increase your awareness. It is important that you are honest with yourself. And again, it's okay if you have these beliefs and biases; you first have to face them to work through them.

Check the box next to the biases you have about queer people and queer life.

○ Queer people are promiscuous.

○ Queer people are just confused.

○ Queer people want attention.

○ Queer people abuse drugs.

○ Children are too young to know they are LGBTQ+.

○ Sexual orientation is a choice.

○ "Changing" your gender is wrong.

○ Children should always be raised by a man and a woman.

○ All queer people have been sexually abused.

○ Queer people are never religious.

○ Queer people are trying to convert others.

○ "Changing" your gender is unnecessary.

How did it feel to acknowledge some of your biases?

_____

_____

_____

_____

_____

_____

_____

_____

Were you surprised by any of your biases? ◯ *Yes* | ◯ *No*

How did you come to have these beliefs about queer people?

_____

_____

_____

_____

_____

_____

_____

_____

_____

_____

Have your beliefs about queer people changed throughout your life? If so, how?

_____

_____

_____

_____

_____

_____

_____

_____

Feelings Are Complicated

This is another exercise to help you build your awareness about your feelings.

Think about your child's coming out (or your learning about their sexual orientation and/or gender identity). **Circle** the feelings that come up for you now, then **underline** the feelings that came up at the time of their coming out.

Joy

Powerlessness

Optimism

Peace

Relief

Shame

Love

Regret

Frustration

Nervousness

Hope

Compassion

Speechlessness

Empathy

Pessimism

Confusion

Loneliness

Shock

Disappointment

Inferiority

Helplessness

Guilt

Happiness

Worry

Sadness

Rage

What was it like for you to acknowledge these feelings?

_____

_____

_____

_____

_____

_____

_____

_____

Which feelings seem to be contradictory?

_____

_____

_____

_____

_____

Which feelings were both circled and underlined? Why do you think those feelings have stayed consistent so far?

_____

_____

_____

_____

_____

_____

Which feelings do you hope will change with time?

_____

_____

_____

_____

_____

_____

_____

_____

Which feelings did change with time (the ones that are underlined but not circled, or vice versa)? Why do you think those feelings changed?

_____

_____

_____

_____

_____

_____

_____

_____

_____

_____

Any and all of the feelings you are experiencing are okay. The key part is that you become aware of those feelings and, with that awareness, you start to process them and make positive changes for your child and yourself.

Facing Your Fears

Since your child's coming out, you have probably experienced some feelings of fear and worry. Let's face it: not having all the answers can be scary. For example, maybe you are worried about what other family members will think, or maybe you are worried about your child's wellness. Any and all of these feelings are okay.

Write down some of those fears, worries, and concerns.

_____

_____

_____

_____

_____

_____

_____

_____

_____

_____

_____

_____

_____

_____

_____

Are the fears you wrote down based on facts? ○ *Yes* | ○ *No*

Write down statements that challenge these fears. Reflect on how likely it is for these fears to occur.

_____

_____

_____

_____

_____

_____

_____

_____

_____

_____

_____

_____

_____

_____

_____

_____

_____

_____

_____

Stages of Grief: From Rainstorms to Rainbows

Many people experience feelings of grief when their child comes out. Some feel like they are mourning their idea of their child, and mourning the future they envisioned for their child. Though your child's coming out is not, in fact, a death, it can help to process your feelings through the lens of the stages of grief.

You might be familiar with the original five stages of grief coined by Elisabeth Kübler-Ross. Over time, different variations have developed (for example, you may hear about the popular seven-stage model). I drew from multiple sources and made some changes of my own to create this eight-stage version, which I find especially helpful in my practice.

Stages 1 and 2: Shock and Denial

Describe any feelings of shock you experienced when your child came out. If you didn't experience shock, write why you think that was.

_____

_____

_____

_____

_____

_____

_____

_____

Describe any feelings of denial you had.

_____

_____

_____

_____

_____

_____

_____

_____

_____

Denial usually involves questioning things. In this case, it could be questioning your child and/or questioning yourself. Write down questions you have or had that have contributed to that feeling of denial.

_____

_____

_____

_____

_____

_____

_____

_____

Have any of the questions written above been voiced to your child? If not, why not? If so, what impact do you believe those questions had?

_____

_____

_____

_____

_____

_____

_____

_____

Stages 3 and 4: Anger and Bargaining

Anger is a broad feeling that can stem from many other feelings and situations. Looking back on your journey since your child came out, when has anger built up for you? Did you have anger towards yourself, your child, the world, or even a higher power?

_____

_____

_____

_____

_____

_____

_____

_____

_____

_____

Bargaining can involve trying to make sense of things and feel in control. When your child came out, it could have looked like questioning "why me?" It could have involved questioning your child's expressed identity or wondering if you could do something to change things. For example, maybe you thought, "What if my child was put in sports? Would that make them straight?" Write about any bargaining you experienced.

_____

_____

_____

_____

_____

_____

_____

_____

Stage 5: Depression

Depression in the context of your child's coming out can look like many things: feeling guilty about how you reacted, worrying about your child, fearing judgment from family and friends, and more.

When your child came out, what was your experience with the depression stage?

_____

_____

_____

_____

_____

_____

_____

_____

_____

_____

_____

_____

_____

Stages 6 and 7: Reconstruction and Acceptance

Reconstruction can look like life starting to get back to normal. Reflect on the things that have stayed the same since your child came out. Write your thoughts and feelings.

_____

_____

_____

_____

_____

_____

_____

_____

_____

_____

In the context of your child's coming out, acceptance can look like understanding that your child's voiced truth and identities are valid. It is completely okay if you are not in this stage; that is why you are working through this book. Write what you hope acceptance will look like for you. If you have already reached acceptance, write about how that feels.

_____

_____

_____

_____

_____

_____

_____

_____

_____

_____

_____

_____

_____

Stage 8: Celebration

This is not one of the traditional stages of grief. I added this one because we want to strive for more than just acceptance. Your child's brave act of coming out should be celebrated. Not only that; your journey of learning and growing should be celebrated.

Write some big and small ways you can celebrate your child's coming out. You might get some ideas from thinking about the five love languages, coined by Gary Chapman: words of affirmation, acts of service, receiving gifts, physical touch, and quality time.

_____

_____

_____

_____

_____

_____

_____

_____

_____

_____

Special Challenge!

Consume a piece of queer media, whether that means searching "LGBTQ+" on streaming platforms, listening to queer playlists or podcasts, or reading a book with a queer protagonist. This could be a great opportunity to ask your kid for recommendations; you could also learn some of their interests in the process. Make sure that you complete this challenge without your child present. (Sneak peek: you will get to do a similar challenge with your child later on.)

Processing

What LGBTQ+ content did you consume?

_____

_____

_____

_____

_____

_____

How would you rate your comfort level while consuming the LGBTQ+ media?

○ *very uncomfortable* ○ *uncomfortable* ○ *neutral* ○ *comfortable* ○ *very comfortable*

Write a summary of the LGBTQ+ media you consumed, then write your thoughts and feelings about the content.

_____

_____

_____

_____

_____

_____

_____

_____

_____

_____

_____

_____

_____

Take a pause.

You are doing great! Take a day or two off from the workbook. It is advised that you take some time to review previous pages and reflect on your progress before moving ahead. Remember, this is a journey, not a race. Use the following space to write down your reflections or take notes for the week.

_____

_____

_____

_____

_____

_____

_____

_____

_____

_____

_____

_____

_____

_____

_____

_____

_____

Week 3: Sexual Orientation, Sex, and Dating

Because we need to talk about it.

or Week 3, the focus will be on sexual orientation, sex, and dating. You will reflect on your own sexuality and your romantic and sexual experiences. There will be a few Let's Talk challenges, which means you will potentially be having some difficult conversations with your child on these topics.

Sex Comfort Assessment

1. I am comfortable discussing my sexual experiences with my friends.

   ○ *strongly disagree* ○ *disagree* ○ *neutral* ○ *agree* ○ *strongly agree*

2. I am comfortable discussing sex with my child.

   ○ *strongly disagree* ○ *disagree* ○ *neutral* ○ *agree* ○ *strongly agree*

3. My current views on sex are shaped by what my parents taught me.

   ○ *strongly disagree* ○ *disagree* ○ *neutral* ○ *agree* ○ *strongly agree*

4. My current views on sex are shaped by my religion.

   ○ *strongly disagree* ○ *disagree* ○ *neutral* ○ *agree* ○ *strongly agree*

5. I think sex should only be between a married couple.

   ○ *strongly disagree* ○ *disagree* ○ *neutral* ○ *agree* ○ *strongly agree*

6. I think sex should only be between people that know and care about each other.

○ *strongly disagree* ○ *disagree* ○ *neutral* ○ *agree* ○ *strongly agree*

7. I am comfortable with the idea of my child having sex.

○ *strongly disagree* ○ *disagree* ○ *neutral* ○ *agree* ○ *strongly agree*

8. I think sex should be pleasurable.

○ *strongly disagree* ○ *disagree* ○ *neutral* ○ *agree* ○ *strongly agree*

How to Calculate Results

Questions 1, 2, 7, and 8

Strongly Disagree: 1 point

Disagree: 2 points

Neutral: 3 points

Agree: 4 points

Strongly Agree: 5 points

Questions 3–6

Strongly Agree: 1 point

Agree: 2 points

Neutral: 3 points

Disagree: 4 points

Strongly Disagree: 5 points

Your result: _____

8–16 points: Sex is a very uncomfortable subject for you. You have a ways to go, but starting the journey is what's most important.

17–27 points: You have some discomfort with sex, but you do have a level of tolerance that can easily be built on.

28–34 points: You are mostly comfortable with sex!

35+ points: You are completely comfortable with sex!

Your results should only be used to increase your self-awareness; they are in no way an indication of your character.

Your Sexuality

Sexuality is much more than just sexual attraction. Sexuality is connected to our bodies, relationships, gender, behaviors, and yes, attraction too.

For the next few pages you will be looking inward and examining your own sexuality. You might not know how to answer some questions, but that is okay; the point is to help you gain a deeper understanding of sexuality.

How would you describe your sexual orientation (e.g., lesbian, pansexual, gay, etc.)?

_____

"My sexual orientation is important to me."

○ *strongly disagree* ○ *disagree* ○ *neutral* ○ *agree* ○ *strongly agree*

"My sexual orientation impacts how people treat me."

○ *strongly disagree* ○ *disagree* ○ *neutral* ○ *agree* ○ *strongly agree*

Write down your thoughts on how your sexual orientation impacts your life.

_____

_____

_____

_____

_____

_____

_____

_____

At what age were you certain of your sexual orientation? _____

Throughout your childhood, was your sexual orientation assumed to be heterosexual? ○ *Yes* | ○ *No*

Prior to your child's coming out, did you assume your child's sexual orientation to be heterosexual? ○ *Yes* | ○ *No*

If you did make assumptions about your child's sexual orientation, how do you think that impacted them?

_____

_____

_____

_____

_____

How do you think it impacts your child when other people make assumptions about their sexual orientation?

_____

_____

_____

_____

Your Ideas about Romance

Society sends countless messages about romance: what it means, what it looks like, even how it "should" feel. This exercise will help you expand your ideas about romance.

How would you define a romantic connection with someone?

_____

_____

_____

Did your definition of a romantic connection include anything sexual?

○ *Yes* | ○ *No*

According to your exact definition of a romantic connection, could a romantic connection occur between two people regardless of their gender identities?

○ *Yes* | ○ *No*

Reflect on the reason for your response to the previous question. Write your thoughts and feelings.

_____

_____

_____

_____

What do you think is more important to the healthiness and happiness of a relationship? ○ *Romantic Connection* | ○ *Sexual Connection*

Describe the kinds of relationships (platonic and/or romantic) you hope your child has in the future.

_____

_____

_____

_____

_____

_____

Reflect on your response to the previous question. Do you think the gender of your child's partner is a crucial part of the kind of relationship you hope your child will have in the future?

○ *Yes* | ○ *No*

Write your thoughts and feelings regarding your response to the previous question.

_____

_____

_____

_____

_____

_____

_____

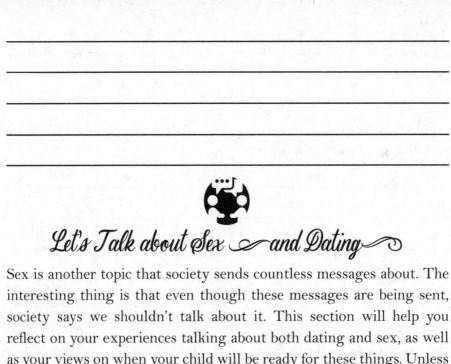

Let's Talk about Sex and Dating

Sex is another topic that society sends countless messages about. The interesting thing is that even though these messages are being sent, society says we shouldn't talk about it. This section will help you reflect on your experiences talking about both dating and sex, as well as your views on when your child will be ready for these things. Unless your child is aromantic, they will most likely date and form romantic relationships. And unless they came out as asexual, it is very likely that they will eventually have sex, or that they already have. (By the way, even if they identify as asexual, there is still a possibility of them having sex.) Therefore, it is important for you to know how to discuss these topics with your child.

Part 1: Dating

Growing up, what were some conversations your parents/guardians had with you about dating?

_____

_____

_____

_____

_____

_____

What do you feel was missing from these conversations about dating? For example, did you want more advice, or less rules and judgment?

_____

_____

_____

How do you think these experiences impacted your views on dating?

_____

_____

_____

_____

Have you had any conversations with your child about dating? If not, why do you think you haven't yet? If you have, how do you think those conversations went?

_____

_____

_____

_____

Did your child's coming out impact your level of comfort with discussing dating with them? If so, how?

_____

_____

_____

_____

Do you believe discussion of dating is an important part of creating an emotionally safe household for your child to express their feelings?
◯ *Yes* | ◯ *No*

Part 2: Sex

Growing up, what were some conversations your parents/guardians had with you about sex?

_____

_____

_____

_____

What do you feel was missing from these conversations about sex? For example, did you want more advice, or less rules and judgment?

_____

_____

_____

_____

_____

How do you think these experiences impacted your views on sex?

_____

_____

_____

_____

Have you had any conversations with your child about sex? If not, why do you think you haven't yet? If you have, how do you think those conversations went?

_____

_____

_____

_____

Did your child's coming out impact your level of comfort with discussing sex with them? If so, how?

_____

_____

_____

_____

_____

Do you believe discussion of sexuality is an important part of creating an emotionally safe household for your child to express their feelings?
○ *Yes* | ○ *No*

After Part 3 of this exercise, we will go over some tips on having conversations about sex and dating with your child.

Part 3: Age and Readiness

At what age did you have your first relationship? _____

At what age did you have your first sexual experience with another?

_____

At what age do you think your child will be "ready" for their first relationship? _____

At what age do you think your child will be "ready" for their first sexual experience with another? _____

Did you write different ages for when you experienced your first relationship and when you think your child will be "ready" for their first relationship? Why or why not? Write your thoughts and feelings.

_____

_____

_____

_____

_____

_____

_____

_____

_____

_____

Did you write different ages for when you had your first sexual experience with another and when you think your child will be "ready" for their first sexual experience with another? Why or why not? Write your thoughts and feelings.

_____

_____

_____

_____

_____

_____

_____

Conversational Templates for Talking with Your Child about Dating and Sex

Before you start, it is important to note that it is okay if your child is not comfortable talking about dating and sex. You can help create a safe space for your child to share by emphasizing that it is okay if they don't feel ready to respond or don't want to respond. Remind your child that the door remains open if they want to revisit the conversation. Use your best judgment on whether to ask some of these questions. For example, if your child is 8 years old, then it might be better to skip some of the questions about dating and sex. However, if your child is 12 years old or older, then it could be helpful to go over all the dating questions and some, if not all, of the sex questions. Regardless of your child's age, make sure to read through all of the questions. These questions should give you a starting point, but don't feel like you need to follow the template exactly; try to let the conversation flow as naturally as possible and tailor your follow-up questions based on your child's responses.

Hey, [insert term of endearment], I want to talk about some things we don't talk much about: sex and dating. Is that okay with you?

I promise that you won't get in trouble for anything you tell me. I just want us to have an open and honest conversation, and I just want to make sure you're safe.

Do you feel comfortable talking with me about dating?

What are your thoughts on dating?

Have you dated before?

If not, at what point would you feel comfortable dating someone?

Is there anyone you know that you would want to date?

Do you feel comfortable talking with me about sex?

What are your thoughts on sex?

Have you had sex before?

If not, at what point do you imagine you would be ready to have sex with someone?

Is there anything I could do to help you feel more comfortable talking with me about dating or sex?

Post-Talk Steps

Based on what you learned from your child when talking to them about dating and sex, you could be feeling a lot of different things.

Let's start with safety. Do you have any concerns about your child's health or safety after talking about dating and sex? Write your concerns below.

_____

_____

_____

_____

_____

_____

Check in with yourself. How were you feeling during the talk? This is a
reminder to refer to your coping skills, if needed.

_____

_____

_____

_____

_____

_____

Are there things that your child shared that you need to learn more
about? If so, write them below.

_____

_____

_____

_____

_____

_____

_____

_____

_____

_____

Take a pause.

You are doing great! Take a day or two off from the workbook. It is advised that you take some time to review previous pages and reflect on your progress before moving ahead. Remember, this is a journey, not a race. Use the following space to write down your reflections or take notes for the week.

_____

_____

_____

_____

_____

_____

_____

_____

_____

_____

_____

_____

_____

_____

_____

_____

_____

_____

Week 4: Identity

Because this is who we are.

W hen a child comes out, they are announcing their awareness of another part of their identity. When a child comes out to a parent, they are also asking for acceptance of their identities, and they are asking to be respected, supported, and loved. This week, you'll learn about and reflect on your own identities, your child's identities, and the importance of identity in general. This will help you gain perspective and understand your child as a whole person, rather than just focusing on their gender or sexuality.

Your Identities

Our identities help shape our stories. They impact how we see the world, how we see ourselves, and, in some cases, how the world sees us. Our identities are influenced by many factors: our experiences, our families, our history, our appearance, and so much more. Identities can even change over time. Over the next few pages, I want you to think about your identities and how those identities impact your life. (We'll skip sexual orientation, which you reflected on last week, and gender identity, which we'll cover next week.)

Economic Class

How would you describe your economic class?

_____

"My economic class is important to me."

○ *strongly disagree* ○ *disagree* ○ *neutral* ○ *agree* ○ *strongly agree*

"My economic class impacts how people treat me."

○ *strongly disagree* ○ *disagree* ○ *neutral* ○ *agree* ○ *strongly agree*

Write down your thoughts and feelings on how your economic class impacts your life.

_____

_____

_____

_____

_____

_____

_____

_____

_____

_____

_____

_____

_____

_____

_____

_____

_____

Religion/Spirituality

How would you describe your religion/spirituality?

_____

"My religion/spirituality is important to me."

○ _strongly disagree_ ○ _disagree_ ○ _neutral_ ○ _agree_ ○ _strongly agree_

"My religion/spirituality impacts how people treat me."

○ _strongly disagree_ ○ _disagree_ ○ _neutral_ ○ _agree_ ○ _strongly agree_

Write down your thoughts and feelings on how your religion/spirituality impacts your life.

_____

_____

_____

_____

_____

_____

_____

_____

_____

_____

_____

_____

_____

_____

_____

_____

_____

Race/Ethnicity

How would you describe your race/ethnicity?

_____

"My race/ethnicity is important to me."

    ○ *strongly disagree* ○ *disagree* ○ *neutral* ○ *agree* ○ *strongly agree*

"My race/ethnicity impacts how people treat me."

    ○ *strongly disagree* ○ *disagree* ○ *neutral* ○ *agree* ○ *strongly agree*

Write down your thoughts and feelings on how your race/ethnicity impacts your life.

_____

_____

_____

_____

_____

_____

_____

_____

_____

_____

_____

_____

_____

_____

_____

_____

_____

Physical/Mental Abilities or Disabilities

How would you describe your physical/mental abilities or disabilities?

_____

"My physical/mental abilities or disabilities are important to me."

    ○ *strongly disagree* ○ *disagree* ○ *neutral* ○ *agree* ○ *strongly agree*

"My physical/mental abilities or disabilities impact how people treat me."

    ○ *strongly disagree* ○ *disagree* ○ *neutral* ○ *agree* ○ *strongly agree*

Write down your thoughts and feelings on how your physical/mental abilities or disabilities impact your life.

_____

_____

_____

_____

_____

_____

_____

_____

_____

_____

_____

_____

_____

_____

_____

_____

_____

Education Level/Profession

How would you describe your education level/profession?

_____

"My education level/profession is important to me."

○ *strongly disagree* ○ *disagree* ○ *neutral* ○ *agree* ○ *strongly agree*

"My education level/profession impacts how people treat me."

○ *strongly disagree* ○ *disagree* ○ *neutral* ○ *agree* ○ *strongly agree*

Write down your thoughts and feelings on how your education level/profession impacts your life.

_____

_____

_____

_____

_____

_____

_____

_____

_____

_____

_____

_____

_____

_____

_____

_____

_____

_____

If a stranger looked at each identity that you wrote individually, they might think they had a pretty good picture of who you are as a person. However, if that person took into account other aspects of your identity, then they would have a more vibrant picture of who you are. For example, learning that a woman has a profession as a lawyer, is Asian, and is poor is much more revealing than just learning someone is a woman.

Your child's coming out means they identify in a new way, whether that's in regards to sexuality, gender identity, or both. How do you think this will impact their life in the present?

_____

_____

_____

_____

_____

_____

How do you think this will impact their life in the next five years?

_____

_____

_____

_____

_____

_____

List the three identities that you feel most emotionally connected to.

_____

_____

_____

_____

_____

List the three identities that you think your child is most emotionally connected to.

_____

_____

_____

_____

_____

_____

_____

Did you list gender identity or sexuality in either list above? Reflect on why or why not and write your thoughts and feelings.

_____

_____

_____

_____

_____

_____

_____

List identities that you typically assume when you meet someone new.

_____

_____

_____

_____

_____

_____

List identities that people sometimes assume about you when they meet you.

_____

_____

_____

_____

_____

_____

_____

Imagine that someone made an incorrect assumption about one of your identities (for example, by incorrectly assuming your race or ethnicity). For which of the identities listed above would this cause feelings of hurt?

_____

_____

_____

_____

_____

_____

Write how you would feel in the scenario listed above (for example, if someone incorrectly assumed your religion, gender, or physical abilities).

_____

_____

_____

_____

_____

_____

_____

_____

Which of the identities do you think would cause feelings of hurt for your child if you incorrectly labeled them with it?

_____

_____

_____

_____

_____

_____

Write how you think your child would feel if someone they cared about incorrectly assumed their identities.

_____

_____

_____

_____

_____

_____

_____

_____

_____

When it comes to people assuming your identities vs. your child's identities, were the feelings you wrote down similar?

○ *Yes* | ○ *No*

In what ways is it different for someone to assume your identities vs. your child's? Do your identities impact how frequently these assumptions are made? Write your thoughts and feelings.

_____

_____

_____

_____

_____

_____

_____

_____

_____

_____

_____

_____

_____

_____

_____

_____

_____

_____

_____

Let's Talk

This week ask your child how they identify. Ask what their most important identities are. After they share, share some of your important identities.

Tips!

It's okay if your child is not comfortable talking about their identities. You can help create a safe space for your child to share by emphasizing that it's okay if they don't feel ready to respond or don't want to respond. Remind your child that the door remains open if they want to revisit the conversation. Also, try not to correct your child; thank them for sharing and ask them how they felt sharing that information. Listen and validate.

Processing

How did your talk with your child go? Were there any surprises? Did you learn anything new about your child?

_____

_____

_____

_____

_____

_____

_____

_____

_____

_____

_____

_____

_____

_____

_____

_____

Write down the identities that your child said were most important to them.

_____

_____

_____

Write what you were thinking and feeling as your child shared information about their identities.

_____

_____

_____

_____

_____

_____

_____

_____

_____

What was it like to share some of your identities with your child? How did they respond?

_____

_____

_____

_____

_____

_____

_____

_____

_____

_____

_____

Timed Worksheet Alert!!

The following page is a timed worksheet. Get your phone out and set your timer to 60 seconds! This includes the time to read the instructions. Start the timer when you turn the page.

Ready . . . set . . . go!!

Timed Worksheet

Write down a list of your child's positive traits.

_____

_____

_____

_____

_____

_____

_____

_____

_____

_____

_____

_____

_____

_____

_____

_____

_____

_____

_____

_____

_____

_____

Processing

What are your own positive traits?

_____

_____

_____

_____

_____

What positive traits do you have in common with your child?

_____

_____

_____

_____

Do you think any of your child's positive traits are connected to your child's sexuality or gender identity? Why or why not?

_____

_____

_____

_____

_____

_____

_____

Many times when a parent learns of their child's sexuality or gender identity, they can become hyper focused on those identities. Sometimes it's good to remember that all of the positive traits your child has will remain the same. In fact, it is likely that you will begin to notice even more positive traits. As you start to build a safer and more accepting environment while progressing through this workbook, your child might start to feel safer expressing their authentic self.

This week focused on your identities and the identities of your child. As you reflect on the week, write down any new insights you have on your child's identities and your own. Have any of your views changed? Why or why not?

_____

_____

_____

_____

_____

_____

_____

_____

_____

_____

_____

_____

_____

_____

_____

Take a pause.

You are doing great! Take a day or two off from the workbook. It is advised that you take some time to review previous pages and reflect on your progress before moving ahead. Remember, this is a journey, not a race. Use the following space to write down your reflections or take notes for the week.

_____

_____

_____

_____

_____

_____

_____

_____

_____

_____

_____

_____

_____

_____

_____

_____

_____

Week 5: Gender Identity and Expression
Because everyone is talking about it.

his week is about gender identity . . . gasp! Our society places gender on so many things that it reaches the level of absurdity. There is gender in colors, clothing, careers, mannerisms, words. . . you get the picture. You simply can't escape it, which is why this part of the workbook is so important. This week will push you to explore the ins and outs of gender identity and help you to expand your views on what gender really is.

Gender Identity

How would you describe your gender identity (e.g., nonbinary, woman)?

_____

"My gender identity is important to me."

○ *strongly disagree* ○ *disagree* ○ *neutral* ○ *agree* ○ *strongly agree*

"My gender identity impacts how people treat me."

○ *strongly disagree* ○ *disagree* ○ *neutral* ○ *agree* ○ *strongly agree*

Write down your thoughts and feelings on how your gender identity impacts your life.

_____

_____

_____

_____

_____

_____

_____

Pronouns

Pronouns are very important: they are part of the way we communicate with each other. Pronouns can be especially important for nonbinary and transgender kids and adults. It is important that you use the correct pronouns when referring to your child. Some studies show that just using the correct pronouns can reduce the risk of suicide significantly for trans and nonbinary kids. A common scenario is when a parent uses the correct pronouns in front of their child but then uses the incorrect ones when they have a mental dialogue going. It is crucial that you try to use the correct pronouns in your mind; that way you can start to internalize and accept your child's gender identity.

Just a reminder to not accidentally out your child to others: it's okay to ask your child what pronouns to use in different environments (school, church, grandparents' house, etc.). If you mess up pronouns in front of your child, it is best to correct yourself, apologize, and try to move on with the conversation, unless your child says otherwise.

Here are some common pronouns:

He/Him

She/Her

They/Them: typically used by nonbinary and gender-nonconforming people

Here are some newer pronouns (neopronouns) used by some:

Ze/Hir (pronounced like "zee" and "here"): another way to refer to someone without expressing gender

Xe/Xir (pronounced like "zee" and "zeer"): another way to refer to someone without expressing gender

Additionally, some people do not have pronouns and prefer to go by their name only.

Ask your child what their pronouns are and write them below:

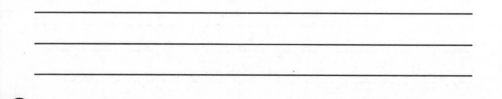

What feelings come up when you think about the idea of using new pronouns for your child? Dig deeper: What do you think is fueling those feelings?

_____

_____

_____

_____

_____

_____

_____

_____

_____

If your child has different pronouns from the ones you have typically used for them, what do you think will be the emotional impact of using the correct pronouns? Do you believe it will have any effect on your child's mental health? Why?

_____

_____

_____

_____

_____

_____

_____

_____

Gender Expression

Gender expression is the way in which you present your gender identity. Common ways to express gender identity are through clothing, voice, hair, and behaviors, but this list is not exhaustive. Gender expression is different from gender identity and is in no way connected to sexuality. Gender expression is typically, but not always, more fluid than gender identity. For example, your gender might be expressed through your clothing based on the setting. Maybe at work you dress more gender neutral with pants and a polo shirt, but if you go to a concert or wedding you dress more feminine by wearing a dress. While your gender expression is more feminine in one setting than the other, your gender identity remains the same.

Your Gender Expression

Keeping in mind your gender identity, what are some components of your gender expression?

Clothing (e.g., dresses, jeans, tank tops):

_____

Hair (e.g., short, long, pink, black, Mohawk, pixie cut):

_____

Voice (e.g., soft, deep, loud):

_____

Pronouns (e.g., he, she, they):

_____

Hobbies and interests (e.g., painting, yoga):

_____

Other types of gender expression:

_____

_____

_____

In what ways is your gender expression in line with societal expectations? For example, are you a man that likes to keep your hair short, or a woman that likes to wear jewelry?

_____

_____

_____

_____

_____

_____

_____

In what ways is your gender expression not in line with societal expectations? For example, are you a woman that likes to fix up cars, or a man that dyes his hair pink?

_____

_____

_____

_____

_____

How has your gender expression changed throughout your life? For example, did you start dressing differently at some point?

_____

_____

_____

_____

How would you react if you were suddenly expected to express your gender in a way that did not align with your gender identity (for example, if you are a man and you were expected to start wearing makeup)?

_____

_____

_____

_____

_____

_____

_____

If you had a wedding to attend and were expected to wear a dress, how would you feel?

_____

_____

_____

_____

_____

If you had a wedding to attend and were expected to wear a suit, how would you feel?

_____

_____

_____

_____

How do you think your child would feel if they were told to wear clothing that did not align with their gender identity? Write your thoughts and feelings.

_____

_____

_____

_____

_____

_____

_____

_____

_____

Think of a past special occasion that you attended with your child. How did they behave? How do you think the clothing they wore affected how they acted?

_____

_____

_____

_____

_____

_____

_____

_____

Your Child's Gender Expression

Write down descriptions of the different components of your child's gender expression.

Clothing (e.g., dresses, jeans, tank tops, etc.):

_____

Hair (e.g., short, long, pink, black, Mohawk, pixie cut, etc.):

_____

Voice (e.g., soft, deep, loud, etc.):

_____

Pronouns (e.g., he, she, they, etc.):

_____

Hobbies and interests (e.g., painting, yoga, etc.):

_____

Other types of gender expression:

_____

_____

_____

_____

_____

_____

Keeping those descriptions in mind, would you describe your child's gender expression as more masculine or more feminine? Or neither?

○ *Masculine* | ○ *Feminine* | ○ *Other*

Do you ever wish you could change all or part of your child's gender expression?

○ *Yes* | ○ *No*

Do you believe your child's gender expression impacts their mental health?

○ *Yes* | ○ *No*

Why or why not? Reflect on how your child's mental health would be if they were forced to express their gender in a different way. Or, if they are currently unable to express their gender freely, reflect on how this might be affecting their mental health. Write down your thoughts and feelings.

_____

_____

_____

_____

_____

_____

_____

Biological vs. Social

Discussion of gender is usually limited to the biological aspects. However, that is a narrow view. In the following pages, you will examine both the biological and social aspects of gender.

Timed Worksheet Alert!!

The following page is a timed worksheet. Get your phone out and set your timer to 60 seconds! This includes the time to read the instructions. Start the timer when you turn the page.

Ready . . . set . . . go!!

Timed Worksheet

Write a list of all the feminine and masculine personality (social) traits you can think of.

Feminine	Masculine

Timed Worksheet Alert!!

The following page is a timed worksheet. Get your phone out and set your timer to 60 seconds! This includes the time to read the instructions. Start the timer when you turn the page.

Ready . . . set . . . go!!

Timed Worksheet

Write a list of all the feminine and masculine biological characteristics you can think of.

Feminine	Masculine

Processing

Which timed exercise was easier for you to complete?

○ *Social* | ○ *Biological*

Which do you think describes your own gender identity better?

○ *Social* | ○ *Biological*

Define what your gender identity is. Give as much detail as possible, including information on your gender expression.

_____

_____

_____

_____

_____

_____

Was your definition of your gender identity similar to the initial definition you wrote at the start of this week?

○ *Yes* | ○ *No*

In what ways was your definition of your gender identity different from your initial definition? In what ways was it the same? Write your thoughts and feelings.

_____

_____

_____

_____

_____

_____

_____

Let's Talk

This challenge could potentially be very difficult. If you find yourself getting very upset, remember that you can hit pause on the conversation and go back to it another time. Please return to the coping skills section at the beginning of this workbook if needed.

For this Let's Talk challenge, you are going to ask your child about their body image in connection to their gender identity.

Ask your child how they feel about their body. Ask them if there is anything they wish to change about their body to feel more comfortable with it.

Tips!

- This could be difficult for your child to talk about. Make sure to check in with them and remind them that they don't have to share if they don't want to.

- Thank your child for sharing. Ask them how they felt sharing that information.

- Listen and validate. Try not to take what they say personally.

- Ask if there is anything you can do to help your child feel more comfortable in their own skin.

- Try not to comment on your child's body, unless they ask. You might be tempted to say something positive to help them feel better. But you could potentially cause harm by commenting on an insecurity.

Processing

Summarize your child's responses to your "Let's Talk" discussion.

_____

_____

_____

_____

_____

_____

_____

_____

Was there anything new you learned about your child? Were you surprised by anything? How did you feel during the discussion? Write your thoughts and feelings.

_____

_____

_____

_____

_____

_____

_____

_____

_____

_____

_____

Special Challenge!

It's time to go shopping! For many queer kids, the journey of accepting and celebrating their identities involves a change in fashion. For some of those queer kids, their parents or guardians are their main barriers to being able to express themselves fully through fashion.

For this challenge, ask your child to pick a clothing store they would like to go to.

Ask them if there is an article of clothing or accessory that they believe you would **not** buy for them.

Follow up with curiosity. Ask them why they think that is.

Ask them if there is clothing that would help them feel more comfortable in their own skin.

If your child identifies an article of clothing, then it is time to go out and buy it with them. If your child does not identify anything, then it is time to go out and look at clothing, if your child is comfortable with that.

It is crucial that you look at both the boys'/men's and the girls'/women's section of the clothing store. Try to buy your child an item of clothing or an accessory, but only if they express an interest in it.

Processing

Write the thoughts and feelings that came up as you were doing this challenge.

_____

_____

_____

_____

_____

_____

_____

_____

Write how you think your child responded to this challenge. Were they embarrassed, excited, annoyed?

_____

_____

_____

_____

_____

What clothing or accessory did you buy? What gendered thoughts did you have about this item?

_____

_____

_____

_____

_____

Write any worries you have about your child wearing this clothing and/or accessory. Are there any safety parameters you want to set with your child around their new clothing (for example, wearing it only in the house or only at school)? Try to reflect on whether you want to create parameters based on safety or because of your own discomfort. This could be a good opportunity to discuss with your child any concerns they have about wearing certain clothing.

_____

_____

_____

_____

_____

_____

_____

_____

_____

_____

_____

_____

_____

_____

_____

_____

_____

_____

_____

_____

You are over halfway through. Congratulations! To wrap up this week, you will list the **three** exercises (worksheets, Let's Talks, and Special Challenges) from the past five weeks that you thought were the most helpful and the **three** exercises that you thought were the most difficult. It is okay if there is overlap.

Most Helpful

_____

_____

_____

_____

_____

_____

_____

Most Difficult

_____

_____

_____

_____

_____

_____

_____

_____

_____

_____

_____

Write down why you thought those exercises were the most helpful and the most difficult, respectively. What do you think this says about your relationship with your child?

_____

_____

_____

_____

_____

_____

_____

_____

_____

_____

_____

_____

_____

_____

_____

_____

_____

_____

_____

_____

_____

_____

_____

Week 6: Your Dreams for Your Child

Because we're all dreamers, aren't we?

T he second a child comes into our lives, many of us start to dream. We start to have hopes for their future. When those dreams start to seem unlikely, it can cause some emotional turmoil. This week is about processing all the feelings that come with your dreams for your child.

Queer Comfort Assessment: Midpoint

Before jumping into this week's content, you will take the Queer Comfort Assessment again to gauge your progress over the past five weeks.

I am comfortable seeing two men kissing on television.

◯ *strongly disagree* ◯ *disagree* ◯ *neutral* ◯ *agree* ◯ *strongly agree*

I am comfortable using "they/them" pronouns for anyone that asks.

◯ *strongly disagree* ◯ *disagree* ◯ *neutral* ◯ *agree* ◯ *strongly agree*

I would be okay with wearing the clothing of a different gender outside.

◯ *strongly disagree* ◯ *disagree* ◯ *neutral* ◯ *agree* ◯ *strongly agree*

I am comfortable going to a pride parade.

◯ *strongly disagree* ◯ *disagree* ◯ *neutral* ◯ *agree* ◯ *strongly agree*

I am comfortable attending a drag show or event.

◯ *strongly disagree* ◯ *disagree* ◯ *neutral* ◯ *agree* ◯ *strongly agree*

I am comfortable going to an LGBTQ+ bar.

◯ *strongly disagree* ◯ *disagree* ◯ *neutral* ◯ *agree* ◯ *strongly agree*

Children are capable of knowing their sexuality.

◯ *strongly disagree* ◯ *disagree* ◯ *neutral* ◯ *agree* ◯ *strongly agree*

I am comfortable with a boy dressing as a Disney princess for Halloween.

○ *strongly disagree* ○ *disagree* ○ *neutral* ○ *agree* ○ *strongly agree*

I am comfortable with trans teens taking hormones to transition (e.g., estrogen or testosterone).

○ *strongly disagree* ○ *disagree* ○ *neutral* ○ *agree* ○ *strongly agree*

I have questioned my own sexuality.

○ *strongly disagree* ○ *disagree* ○ *neutral* ○ *agree* ○ *strongly agree*

I have questioned my own gender identity.

○ *strongly disagree* ○ *disagree* ○ *neutral* ○ *agree* ○ *strongly agree*

How to Calculate Results

Strongly disagree: 1 point

Disagree: 2 points

Neutral: 3 points

Agree: 4 points

Strongly agree: 5 points

Your result: _____

11–27 points: Heteronormality has made queerness very uncomfortable for you. You have a ways to go, but starting the journey is what's most important.

28–39 points: You have some discomfort with queerness, but you do have a level of tolerance that can easily be built on.

40–49 points: You are mostly comfortable with queerness. More exposure will lead to a lot of growth.

50+ points: You are completely comfortable with queerness!

Your results should only be used to increase your self-awareness; they are in no way an indication of your character.

Processing

Look back at your initial Queer Comfort Assessment results. Were there any changes? What do you think is needed for you to make more progress? Write down your thoughts and feelings.

_____

_____

_____

_____

_____

_____

_____

_____

_____

_____

_____

_____

_____

_____

_____

_____

_____

_____

_____

_____

_____

_____

Special Challenge!

Part 1

Write a magical fantasy story about your child's life 20 years from now. It's important for it to be written as a magical fantasy because this helps decrease the chances of any triggers occuring for you or your child. You will end up sharing your story with your child, and because it won't be based on real life, your child will be less likely to internalize any messages about your expectations, such as what career you envision them having. The focus of this challenge is connection and understanding. Write where your child will live (in a castle, on a cloud, in a volcano, etc.), what their profession will be (knight, wizard, mermaid, etc.), what pets they will have (dragon, fox, gryphon, etc.), and any other fun details you can think of. Try to paint a happy and positive picture. Make sure you do not include any pronouns or information about their relationship status.

_____

_____

_____

_____

_____

_____

_____

_____

_____

_____

_____

Part 2

Share your story with your child and ask them which parts they would change and why. Rewrite the story based on your child's edit.

_____

_____

_____

_____

_____

_____

_____

_____

_____

_____

_____

_____

_____

_____

_____

_____

_____

_____

_____

Processing

What were some of the differences between your original story and the rewrite?

_____

_____

_____

_____

_____

_____

_____

_____

Write your thoughts and feelings about the edits your child made.

_____

_____

_____

_____

_____

_____

_____

_____

_____

_____

Which story do you think would lead to a happier life for your child?

○ *Original Story* | ○ *Rewritten Story*

Write your thoughts and feelings on your response to the previous question.

_____

_____

_____

_____

_____

_____

_____

Reframing Your Dreams

The second your child is born, you begin to dream of their future. Will your son be a track star? Will your daughter be a professional MMA fighter? However, when your child comes out, it can feel like so many of those dreams are slipping away. As we learned in Week 2, grief isn't just about the feelings that come from a loved one passing; here, we'll explore how you can grieve your dreams too.

Write down some dreams you have for your child's future.

_____

_____

_____

_____

_____

_____

_____

_____

_____

_____

_____

Write the dreams that have changed since your child came out.

_____

_____

_____

_____

_____

_____

_____

_____

_____

_____

Write the dreams that have stayed the same since your child came out.

_____

_____

_____

_____

_____

_____

_____

_____

_____

_____

_____

_____

_____

Have there been other times in your child's life when you've questioned or adjusted the dreams you had for them? If so, when?

_____

_____

_____

_____

_____

_____

_____

_____

Where did your dreams for your child come from? Why do you think these dreams came to be? Write your thoughts and feelings.

_____

_____

_____

_____

_____

_____

_____

_____

_____

_____

_____

_____

What about your dreams for yourself? How did they come to be? Who helped influence them? Write your thoughts and feelings.

_____

_____

_____

_____

_____

_____

_____

_____

Write the dreams that have changed throughout your life. Do you feel the changes were positive? Write your thoughts and feelings.

_____

_____

_____

_____

_____

_____

_____

_____

_____

_____

Major Life Event Checklist

Since learning about your child's gender identity and/or sexuality, you may have questions about how it will impact their childhood and the rest of their life. This exercise will help answer those questions.

Next to each life event, if you have experienced it, write the age you were when the event occurred for you.

Passing the driver's test _____

Getting a high school diploma _____

Going to prom _____

Learning to ride a bike _____

Getting your first job _____

Leaving for college _____

Renting your first apartment _____

Buying your first house _____

Graduating college _____

Buying your first car _____

Going to your first wedding _____

Getting married _____

Having your first child _____

Taking a trip abroad _____

Flying on an airplane _____

Learning how to swim _____

Going through your first break-up _____

First time in therapy _____

First kiss _____

Knowing your sexual orientation _____

Knowing your gender identity _____

Solely based on the ages in your completed timeline, which life event "should" your child go through next?

_____

Did your sexuality and/or gender identity have an impact on when you went through the life event that your child "should" go through next (based on your timeline)?

○ *Yes* | ○ *No*

Do you believe your child's sexuality and/or gender identity will have an impact on their next life event (based on your timeline)?

○ *Yes* | ○ *No*

Write your thoughts and feelings about your responses to the previous questions.

_____

_____

_____

_____

_____

_____

_____

_____

_____

_____

_____

Next to each life event, write the age your child would need to be for you to feel comfortable with them going through that experience.

Passing the driver's test _____

Getting a high school diploma _____

Going to prom _____

Learning to ride a bike _____

Getting their first job _____

Leaving for college _____

Renting their first apartment _____

Buying their first house _____

Graduating college _____

Buying their first car _____

Going to their first wedding _____

Getting married _____

Having their first child _____

Taking a trip abroad _____

Flying on an airplane _____

Learning how to swim _____

Going through their first break-up _____

First time in therapy _____

First kiss _____

Knowing their sexual orientation _____

Knowing their gender identity _____

List the major life events that you experienced at a different age from the age at which you are comfortable with your child experiencing them.

_____

_____

_____

_____

_____

_____

_____

_____

_____

What do you think are the reasons for these differences?

_____

_____

_____

_____

_____

_____

_____

_____

_____

_____

_____

_____

Write the major life events that you are most worried about your child experiencing. Next to each one, write whether the concern is about their physical and/or emotional safety.

_____

_____

_____

_____

_____

_____

_____

Write down positive self-talk that challenges the worries you have about your child's physical and emotional safety. For example, if you are worried about your child driving, you might write, "Cars are very safe and I will make sure that my child knows the importance of wearing a seatbelt."

_____

_____

_____

_____

_____

_____

Which three major life events do you think are the most important?

_____

_____

_____

Picture your child achieving your top three major life events. Do any of those pictures change due to your child's coming out?

○ *Yes* | ○ *No*

If yes, write how your picture of your child's future changes. If no, write why you believe the picture stays the same.

_____

_____

_____

_____

_____

_____

_____

_____

_____

_____

_____

_____

_____

_____

_____

_____

_____

Take a pause.

You are doing great! Take a day or two off from the workbook. It is advised that you take some time to review previous pages and reflect on your progress before moving ahead. Remember, this is a journey, not a race. Use the following space to write down your reflections or take notes for the week.

_____

_____

_____

_____

_____

_____

_____

_____

_____

_____

_____

_____

_____

_____

_____

_____

_____

_____

Week 7: Connecting with Your Kid

Because they're still your kid.

Your relationship with your child might have changed a bit since you learned they were queer. This week will help you strengthen your relationship through exercises related to love and connection.

Defining Love

It's obvious that you love your child. That's why you started this workbook. In this section, you will process what that love means and looks like. Start by reflecting on your childhood. How did your parents/guardians show you love when you were growing up? It might help to reflect again on Chapman's five love languages (words of affirmation, acts of service, receiving gifts, physical touch, and quality time).

_____

_____

_____

_____

_____

_____

_____

_____

_____

_____

_____

Are there any ways you think you would have received love better from your parents/guardians (e.g., more hugs, more quality time together, more praise, etc.)?

_____

_____

_____

_____

_____

_____

_____

Now write about the ways in which you show your child love.

_____

_____

_____

_____

_____

_____

_____

_____

_____

_____

_____

_____

Which of your ways of showing your child love are similar to how your parents showed you love?

_____

_____

_____

_____

_____

_____

_____

_____

Which of your ways of showing your child love are different from how your parents showed you love?

_____

_____

_____

_____

_____

_____

_____

_____

_____

_____

Reflecting back on your previous answers, do you think there are ways you can make adjustments to how you show your child love?

_____

_____

_____

_____

_____

_____

_____

_____

_____

_____

_____

_____

_____

_____

_____

_____

_____

_____

_____

_____

Timed Worksheet Alert!!

The following page is a timed worksheet. Get your phone out and set your timer to 60 seconds! This includes the time to read the instructions. Start the timer when you turn the page.

Ready . . . set . . . go!!

Timed Worksheet

There are so many different components to raising a physically and emotionally healthy child. Write down some of your child's physical and emotional needs.

Physical Needs	Emotional Needs

Processing

What did you notice about the needs that you stated in your last answer? For example, do they have anything in common? Did you write down more physical needs or more emotional needs?

_____

_____

_____

_____

_____

_____

_____

_____

Now that you have more time to think, write down any additional needs that you couldn't think of before.

_____

_____

_____

_____

_____

_____

_____

_____

_____

_____

Which of your child's needs do you want to do a better job of meeting?

_____

_____

_____

_____

_____

_____

_____

_____

When a child takes the brave step of sharing their sexual orientation and/or gender identity, it can have a big impact on your relationship with them. However, it usually doesn't impact their emotional needs. Which emotional needs do you think are most important to help your child feel supported during this time?

_____

_____

_____

_____

_____

_____

_____

_____

_____

Let's Talk

For this challenge, you are going to ask your child for feedback on your parenting.

Ask your child how you could improve as a parent. Ask them if they feel that you spend enough time together. Ask them if they feel comfortable sharing their feelings.

Tips!

Thank your child for sharing. Ask them how they felt sharing that information. Listen and validate. Try not to take what they say personally. Do not defend yourself; work on solutions.

Processing

Summarize your child's answers to your Let's Talk questions, then write your thoughts and feelings about their responses.

_____

_____

_____

_____

_____

_____

_____

_____

_____

_____

_____

_____

_____

_____

_____

_____

_____

_____

_____

_____

_____

Have you ever asked your child for feedback on your parenting before?

○ *Yes* | ○ *No*

Have you ever had the chance to give your parents feedback?

○ *Yes* | ○ *No*

If so, how did that go?

_____

_____

_____

_____

_____

_____

_____

_____

_____

_____

_____

_____

_____

_____

_____

_____

_____

_____

_____

_____

_____

Special Challenge!

This Special Challenge is a great way to have fun with your child, especially after the difficult Let's Talk you just had. Ask your child to decide on a physical activity to do together (yoga, walking, weight lifting, swimming, etc.). Remember to give them the option to opt out if they are not comfortable doing a physical activity with you. But if they do choose one, do the activity with them and pay close attention to how your child responds to the exercise.

Processing

What was it like for you to exercise with your child? If your child opted out, how did you feel and why do you think they opted out?

_____

_____

_____

_____

_____

_____

_____

_____

_____

_____

_____

_____

_____

_____

_____

_____

_____

_____

_____

_____

_____

_____

_____

_____

What did you notice about your child during the physical activity? Try to write at least one positive thing and one concern you noticed. Did they show any discomfort with their clothing? Why do you think that is?

_____

_____

_____

_____

_____

_____

_____

All the Colors of the Rainbow

When a child comes out, parents tend to focus on their child's gender identity and sexuality, while losing sight of other things about their child. This exercise is to remind you that your kid is still your kid. Write down answers to these questions about your child.

Favorite color? _____

Ice cream or cookies? _____

Favorite subject in school? _____

Best friend's name? _____

Least favorite teacher's name? _____

Favorite holiday? _____

TV shows or movies? _____

Favorite board game? _____

Which power: super strength or flight? _____

Favorite food for breakfast? _____

Favorite music artist? _____

Favorite activity to do with a parent? _____

Special Challenge!

This week we are cooking! Ask your child if they would like to cook or bake something together. Agree on what to make, then agree on a recipe you want to follow. Finally, decide on one or two ingredients to change or add. After you enjoy your meal, discuss with your child what they thought about the process and the meal.

You might be wondering why you are cooking and why you have to change some of the ingredients. This challenge is about adjusting your expectations. We expect our food will taste a certain way based on the ingredients, but it could end up tasting the same or even better when the ingredients are changed. Similarly, you might have certain expectations for your child, but when you have to change some of these expectations based on their coming out, you might be pleasantly surprised with the result. Learning about your child's sexuality and/or gender identity is kind of like cooking with a new recipe, and even if the end result is not what you expected, most of the time it is just fun to go through the process.

Processing

How was this challenge? Was it better than expected? Was it hard to decide on the ingredients to change? Did this inspire you to cook or bake more or to change your process?

Write your thoughts and feelings.

_____

_____

_____

_____

_____

_____

_____

Did changing or adding new ingredients take away the enjoyment of the cooking or baking process? Why or why not? Write your thoughts and feelings.

_____

_____

_____

_____

_____

_____

_____

_____

_____

_____

Write down some hobbies, interests, and/or traits your child has that you did not expect they would have when they were much younger.

_____

_____

_____

_____

_____

_____

_____

_____

_____

_____

Looking at the list you wrote above, are you glad your child has those hobbies, interests, and/or traits? What would you change about your child? What would you keep the same? Why?

_____

_____

_____

_____

_____

_____

_____

_____

_____

As of right now, how would you describe the connection you have with your child?

_____

_____

_____

_____

_____

_____

_____

_____

Reflecting on just the last month, what do you think has had the biggest positive impact on your connection with your child?

_____

_____

_____

_____

_____

_____

_____

Write down any changes you have noticed in your child's comfort expressing their gender identity and/or sexuality. What do you think has contributed to those changes?

_____

_____

_____

_____

_____

_____

_____

Write any ideas you have about creating an even safer space for your child to be themselves.

_____

_____

_____

_____

_____

_____

_____

_____

_____

_____

Write any ideas you have about how you can increase your comfort with your child's gender identity and/or sexuality. Should you revisit any of the past Special Challenges or Let's Talk exercises?

_____

_____

_____

Take a pause.

You are doing great! Take a day or two off from the workbook. It is advised that you take some time to review previous pages and reflect on your progress before moving ahead. Remember, this is a journey, not a race. Use the following space to write down your reflections or take notes for the week.

_____

_____

_____

_____

_____

_____

_____

_____

_____

_____

_____

_____

_____

_____

_____

_____

_____

_____

_____

_____

Week 8: Your Community

Because no one can go it alone.

Community is an integral part of our mental well-being. The ways in which community impacts well-being vary from person to person. Some people rely mostly on their friends and family, while others might depend more on clubs and organizations. For queer youth, community can have an even more profound effect on their mental health. Having spaces in which they feel safe, both physically and emotionally, is important. This week you will focus on your and your child's community, and ways to create a safer and healthier support system for both of you.

Let's Talk

Queer youth tend to have LGBTQ+ friends because it is a way to feel safer at school, both physically and emotionally. Unfortunately, it is not always easy or possible for kids to find queer friends, which can lead to feelings of loneliness and mental health challenges. This week, ask your child if they have any friends that are queer. If you already know the answer, ask for more details, such as, "How did you find out your friend was queer?"

Processing

What was your main takeaway from your discussion with your child?
Did you learn anything? Was your child comfortable sharing with you?
Write your thoughts and feelings.

_____

_____

_____

_____

_____

_____

_____

_____

_____

_____

_____

_____

_____

_____

_____

_____

_____

_____

_____

Unacceptance

This prompt has a high potential for being triggering based on your life experiences. Make sure to take note of your physical and emotional responses and use the appropriate coping skills.

Reflect on your relationships (friends, family, co-workers, etc.). Write down any significant moments when you felt unaccepted or even rejected by someone you cared about.

_____

_____

_____

_____

_____

_____

_____

What did you notice about those moments of unacceptance? Did they come from some people more than others? Were there more or fewer than you thought there would be?

_____

_____

_____

_____

_____

_____

_____

_____

Were there certain people or groups that you turned to after these moments of unacceptance? If not, what would have been helpful in your community during these moments?

_____

_____

_____

_____

_____

_____

_____

_____

_____

_____

What sort of community support do you think will be helpful for your child after they experience moments of unacceptance?

_____

_____

_____

_____

_____

_____

_____

_____

Family and Friends

When a child comes out, there might be a moment when you think, "What will my _____ think?" This section will help you process and organize some of your thoughts and feelings surrounding your child's coming out and how it impacts your relationships with your friends and family. At the end of this section, you will find some tips on this topic that might be helpful.

List any close family members or friends that are part of the LGBTQ+ community:

_____

_____

_____

_____

List any close family members or friends that are **not** part of the LGBTQ+ community:

_____

_____

_____

_____

List any close family members or friends that advocate for and/or support the LGBTQ+ community:

_____

_____

_____

_____

List any close family members or friends that have made negative statements about the LGBTQ+ community:

_____

_____

Does your child come into contact with any of the people you listed?

◯ *Yes* | ◯ *No*

Have you shared with your child which family and friends would be supportive of their sexuality or gender identity?

◯ *Yes* | ◯ *No*

If your child came out to one of your friends or family members, how do you think you would feel?

_____

_____

_____

_____

_____

_____

If a friend or family member said something homophobic or transphobic around your child, how do you think you would feel?

_____

_____

_____

_____

_____

How do you think your child would feel?

_____

_____

_____

_____

_____

_____

What are some ideas you have for keeping your child emotionally safe from friends or family members that are not supportive of the LGBTQ+ community?

_____

_____

_____

_____

_____

_____

_____

_____

Tips!

- The most important thing is to respect your child's privacy about their identity. It is crucial that you **do not** tell others about your child's sexuality or gender identity without your child's permission.

- Ask your child if any family members do or say things that make them uncomfortable.

What to Say When People Make Bigoted Comments

Before we dive into how to respond, it is important to take note of who is saying these harmful words. Some questions to ask yourself first:

1. Do I think there is a risk to my safety or my child's safety?

2. Is this someone that will be around my child in the future?

3. Is this someone that will be around me but not my child in the future (perhaps a co-worker or friend)?

4. Do I know whether this person is aware that these words are harmful?

5. Do I think they would be open to learning and growing?

6. Is it worth my emotional energy right now?

Every situation is different, and the questions above can help you decide on the best path forward. For example, hearing a family member say something transphobic in your presence requires a different approach compared to reading a transphobic comment on social media (even if the comment was from that same family member). The main focus should be on creating a safe environment for your child, and sometimes addressing a bigoted comment is not the safest path forward. There may be situations in which something is said in front of your child and they don't want you to respond; there might be other times when they will want you to respond. This topic involves consistently checking in with them.

Below are some go-to responses you can use when someone makes a bigoted comment:

"Please don't say that around me."

"I am not comfortable with this topic. Let's change the subject."

"Don't talk about my child like that."

"What you just said really hurt my feelings."

"That is harmful language you are using."

"I do not tolerate hateful messages."

If you want more tips, the University of Houston has put together a great resource on how to respond to homophobia and transphobia with the B.A.R. (Breathe Acknowledge Respond) method:

uh.edu/lgbtq/resources/_files/responding-to-homophobia-with-bar.pdf

Community Resources

Connecting with a safe and accepting community is one of the best ways to support your child's mental health.

Research local pro-LGBTQ+ organizations, support groups, and events (in person or virtual) and write them below. For each one, specify whether it is tailored more towards you, your child, or both.

_____

_____

_____

_____

_____

_____

_____

_____

_____

Of the organizations, support groups, and events that you listed above, which would you be interested in participating in and why? Write how you think you and/or your child could benefit from participating.

_____

_____

_____

_____

_____

_____

_____

_____

Share your list of pro-LGBTQ+ organizations, support groups, and events with your child. Write down any that your child is interested in joining.

_____

_____

_____

_____

_____

_____

If your child is interested in joining or attending any of the organizations, support groups, or events, make a plan with them to do so. If there are any you would like to join or attend yourself, then make a plan for that too. You don't have to carry out your plan this week; there could potentially be weeks or months before you and/or your child can attend.

Special Challenge!

Read the instructions for this challenge, then check in with your child to get permission before trying it.

This week you're going to show your allyship! Display something (or a few things) in your home to show your support for the LGBTQ+ community. Sometimes when a child comes out, they can doubt their family members' support, regardless of what their family members say. This will be a constant visual reminder of your support. If your child is not comfortable with you doing this (which is perfectly okay), then maybe you can put something up in a space where only you go, like your closet or office.

Bonus points if you look up the flag that matches the identity your child came out with.

Processing

Do you feel comfortable putting up a visual reminder of your support for the LGBTQ+ community?

○ *Yes* | ○ *No*

Try to explain where the comfort or discomfort comes from.

_____

_____

_____

_____

_____

_____

_____

_____

_____

What do you think will be the emotional impact on your child if you complete this Special Challenge?

_____

_____

_____

_____

_____

_____

_____

_____

Take a pause.

You are doing great! Take a day or two off from the workbook. It is advised that you take some time to review previous pages and reflect on your progress before moving ahead. Remember, this is a journey, not a race. Use the following space to write down your reflections or take notes for the week.

_____

_____

_____

_____

_____

_____

_____

_____

_____

_____

_____

_____

_____

_____

_____

Week 9: Growth and Reflections

Because you've come a long way.

Over the past eight weeks, you've probably encountered some challenging material and experienced a lot of growth. The final week of this workbook is dedicated to reflecting on your journey so far, as well as thinking about where you'll go from here.

We All Make Mistakes

While completing this workbook, you have probably experienced some feelings of guilt or shame. These next few pages are for trying to accept and forgive yourself.

What are some everyday challenges of parenting for you?

_____

_____

_____

_____

_____

_____

_____

_____

_____

_____

_____

_____

Throughout life, we all make too many mistakes to count, especially as parents. What are some parenting mistakes you have made?

_____

_____

_____

_____

_____

_____

_____

_____

What are some mistakes your own parents/guardians made while raising you?

_____

_____

_____

_____

_____

_____

_____

_____

_____

_____

If you have been able to forgive them for these mistakes, how did you go about it? If you haven't forgiven them, what would they need to do to help you with the process of forgiveness?

_____

_____

_____

_____

_____

_____

_____

_____

_____

_____

_____

_____

Dear Soon-to-Be Parent

Write a letter to your younger self; make sure you date it exactly one week before you started raising your child. What wishes do you have for your younger self? Would you want to warn yourself of something related to parenting? What are some differences between you then and you now? Are you grateful for any choices you made? What did you need to hear from someone back then? You do not need to address all of these questions; the most important part of this exercise is to give your younger self forgiveness for their future mistakes. End the letter with some hope for the future.

Dear _____,   Date _____

_____

_____

_____

_____

_____

_____

_____

_____

_____

_____

_____

_____

_____

_____

_____

_____

_____

_____

_____

_____

_____

_____

_____

Special Challenge!

Consume a piece of queer media **with** your child, whether that means searching "LGBTQ+" on streaming platforms, listening to queer playlists or podcasts, or reading a book with queer protagonists. You and your child can decide on the media together. Do not ambush your child; give them time to think and decide on a day and time to complete the challenge with you.

Processing

What LGBTQ+ content did you consume?

_____

_____

_____

_____

_____

How would you rate your comfort level while consuming the LGBTQ+ media?

○ *very uncomfortable* ○ *uncomfortable* ○ *neutral* ○ *comfortable* ○ *very comfortable*

Was it less comfortable due to your child being there with you? Why or why not?

_____

_____

_____

_____

_____

_____

_____

_____

_____

_____

_____

What was your overall experience of consuming queer media with your child?

_____

_____

_____

_____

_____

_____

Write down what you think your child's experience was like.

_____

_____

_____

_____

_____

Is this Special Challenge something you can see yourself continuing after you complete the workbook? Why or why not?

_____

_____

_____

_____

_____

_____

_____

Your Growth

Which exercise(s) in the workbook was/were most difficult to complete? Write your thoughts and feelings.

_____

_____

_____

_____

_____

_____

_____

_____

_____

_____

_____

_____

_____

_____

_____

_____

_____

_____

Which Special Challenge was the easiest to complete? Write your thoughts and feelings.

_____

_____

_____

_____

_____

_____

_____

_____

_____

Which Let's Talk exercise was the easiest to complete? Write your thoughts and feelings.

_____

_____

_____

_____

_____

_____

_____

_____

_____

Queer Comfort Assessment: Endpoint

You will now complete the assessment a final time to see if any of your answers have changed.

I am comfortable seeing two men kissing on television.

○ *strongly disagree* ○ *disagree* ○ *neutral* ○ *agree* ○ *strongly agree*

I am comfortable using "they/them" pronouns for anyone that asks.

○ *strongly disagree* ○ *disagree* ○ *neutral* ○ *agree* ○ *strongly agree*

I would be okay with wearing the clothing of a different gender outside.

○ *strongly disagree* ○ *disagree* ○ *neutral* ○ *agree* ○ *strongly agree*

I am comfortable going to a pride parade.

○ *strongly disagree* ○ *disagree* ○ *neutral* ○ *agree* ○ *strongly agree*

I am comfortable attending a drag show or event.

○ *strongly disagree* ○ *disagree* ○ *neutral* ○ *agree* ○ *strongly agree*

I am comfortable going to an LGBTQ+ bar.

○ *strongly disagree* ○ *disagree* ○ *neutral* ○ *agree* ○ *strongly agree*

Children are capable of knowing their sexuality.

○ *strongly disagree* ○ *disagree* ○ *neutral* ○ *agree* ○ *strongly agree*

I am comfortable with a boy dressing as a Disney princess for Halloween.

○ *strongly disagree* ○ *disagree* ○ *neutral* ○ *agree* ○ *strongly agree*

I am comfortable with trans teens taking hormones to transition (e.g., estrogen or testosterone).

○ *strongly disagree* ○ *disagree* ○ *neutral* ○ *agree* ○ *strongly agree*

I have questioned my own sexuality.

○ *strongly disagree* ○ *disagree* ○ *neutral* ○ *agree* ○ *strongly agree*

I have questioned my own gender identity.

○ *strongly disagree* ○ *disagree* ○ *neutral* ○ *agree* ○ *strongly agree*

How to Calculate Results

Strongly disagree: 1 point

Disagree: 2 points

Neutral: 3 points

Agree: 4 points

Strongly agree: 5 points

Your result: _____

11–27 points: Heteronormality has made queerness very uncomfortable for you. You have a ways to go, but starting the journey is what's most important.

28–39 points: You have some discomfort with queerness, but you do have a level of tolerance that can easily be built on.

40–49 points: You are mostly comfortable with queerness. More exposure will lead to a lot of growth.

50+ points: You are completely comfortable with queerness!

Your results should only be used to increase your self-awareness; they are in no way an indication of your character.

Processing

Look back at your initial and midpoint Queer Comfort Assessment results. Were there any changes? What do you think is needed for you to make more progress as you come to the end of this workbook? Write down your thoughts and feelings.

_____

_____

_____

_____

_____

_____

_____

_____

_____

Write down the most important things you've learned over the course of this journey.

_____

_____

_____

_____

_____

_____

_____

_____

Was there anything that surprised you about this journey? If so, what?

_____

_____

_____

_____

_____

_____

_____

_____

_____

_____

In what ways did your relationship with your child change or not change throughout this journey?

_____

_____

_____

_____

_____

_____

_____

_____

_____

_____

_____

Shifting towards the future, what are some goals you have for yourself as you continue your journey of growth beyond this workbook?

_____

_____

_____

_____

_____

_____

_____

_____

_____

What do you wish your relationship with your child will look like five years from now?

_____

_____

_____

_____

_____

_____

_____

_____

_____

_____

What is one piece of advice you want to write down to remind yourself of in the future?

_____

_____

_____

_____

_____

_____

_____

_____

_____

_____

_____

_____

_____

_____

_____

_____

_____

_____

_____

_____

Conclusion: Beyond the Ninth Week

You are officially at the end of this workbook. You made it! Time to celebrate all the hard work you've put in. I hope you found this journey both challenging and fun. This is important and meaningful work: any change that happens within you also impacts those around you. You worked to create a more loving and safe environment for your child. You did a deep dive into your own psyche and came out with an expanded way of thinking and being. The focus isn't on the amount of growth you've experienced, though I hope you feel you've grown a lot. The key is that your queer kid feels more connected to you and accepted by you. The world outside might be hateful and hostile towards your child, but at the very least, you can help them feel safer with you.

And that's more important now than ever. As of the 2023 legislative session, the ACLU was tracking **491 anti-LGBTQ+ bills in the United States, 72 of which had been passed into law.** Some states are passing laws that would make it illegal for children to get gender-affirming medical care. It is important that you stay up-to-date on the anti-LGBTQ+ bills being introduced in your state, because these are laws that your child could read about, hear about, or even be directly impacted by. When your child learns of these anti-LGBTQ+ laws, it can have a negative effect on their mental health. They could begin to internalize messages that say that they are less than, that they are immoral, that they are wrong, or that they need to change. This can cause depression, anxiety, low self-esteem, trauma responses, and more mental health battles. To stay up-to-date, you can visit this map put together by the ACLU: https://www.aclu.org/legislation-affecting-lgbtq-rights-across-country. The website is updated weekly.

Aside from staying informed, you might be wondering what else you can do now that you've finished this workbook. Well, you can take what you've learned and continue to build on it. You can continue to be intentional about communicating with your child with curiosity and openness. You can continue to question the messages society sends you about how you "should" be versus how you are or want to be. Now that you view the world through a kaleidoscope of colors, it's almost impossible to go back to gray. All you need to do is keep trying.

About the Author

Marc Campbell is a licensed mental health counselor in the state of Florida. He has worked in the counseling field for over five years. He is a part of the LGBTQ+ community and has experience working directly with LGBTQ+ youth, many of whom were homeless. As an LMHC, he had the unique experience of working as a middle school counselor, where he fought to start the first LGBTQ+ support group at a rural middle school in Central Florida. He was a panelist for Equality Florida's All Together Now Conference, which aims to secure safe learning environments for LGBTQ+ students. He was a guest speaker on communication skills and body positivity for the Bros in Convo Initiative, a Black Queer–led grassroots organization focused on building community by educating and empowering queer people of color in Central Florida. He was also on the Social Justice Panel for the Central Florida Association for Marriage and Family Therapy. His lived experience being a Black Queer licensed mental health counselor gives him a unique lens to write a workbook for parents on how to better support their queer children. Follow Marc on Instagram @mentalhealthwithmarc.

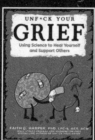

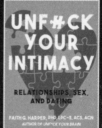